STECK

NEW WAY

HEADS and TAILS

Tug the Rug

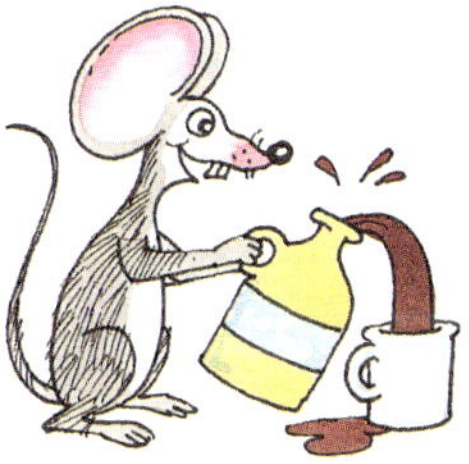

STECK-VAUGHN
COMPANY

A Division of Harcourt Brace & Company

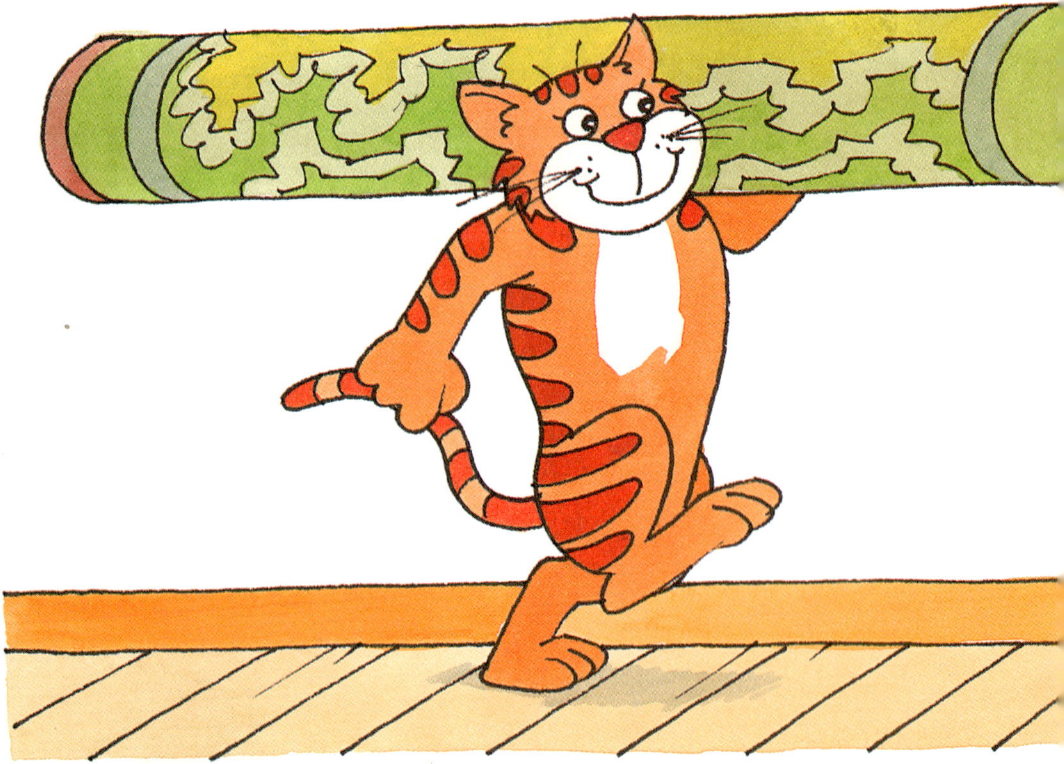

a rug

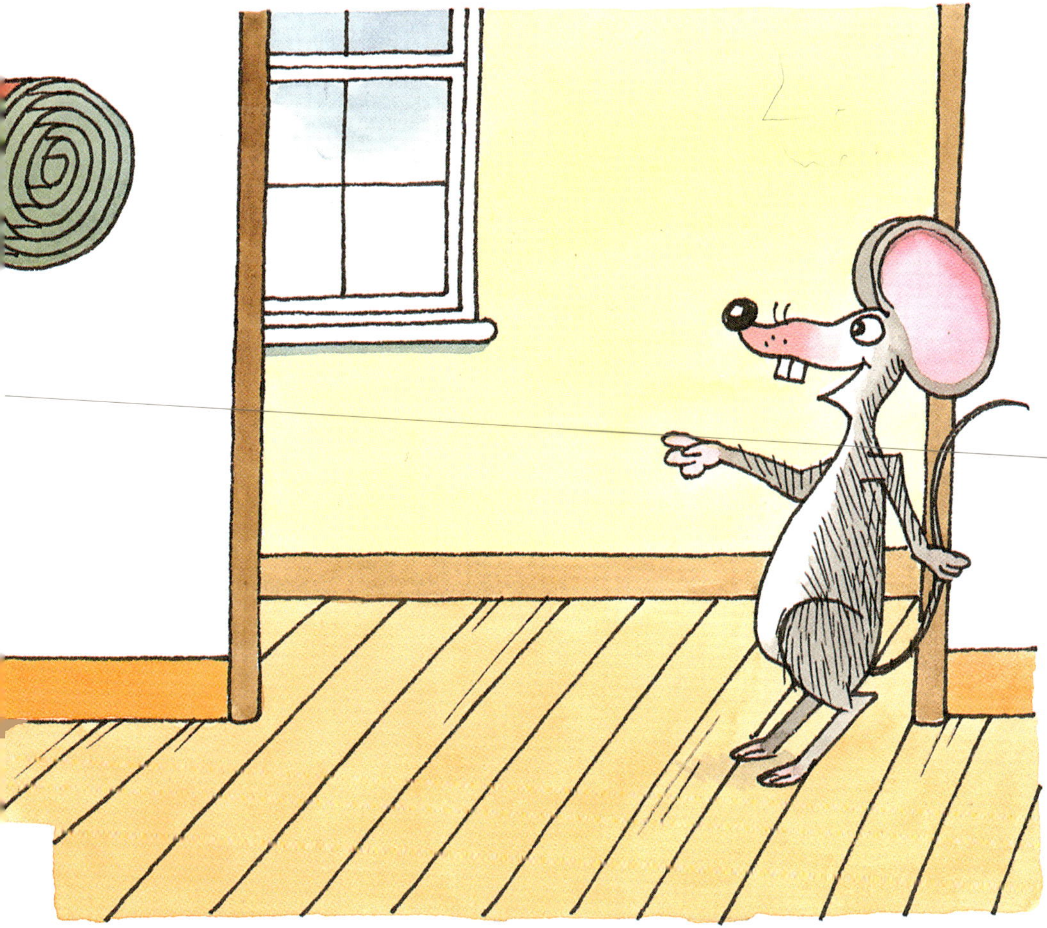

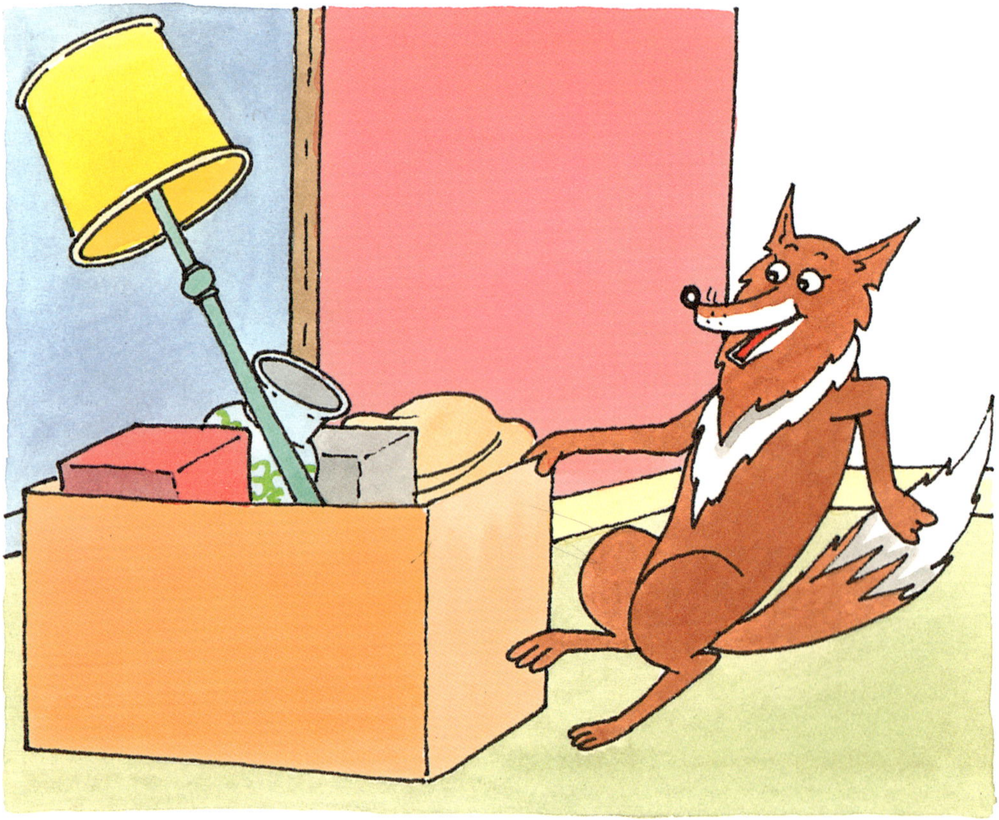

a tug

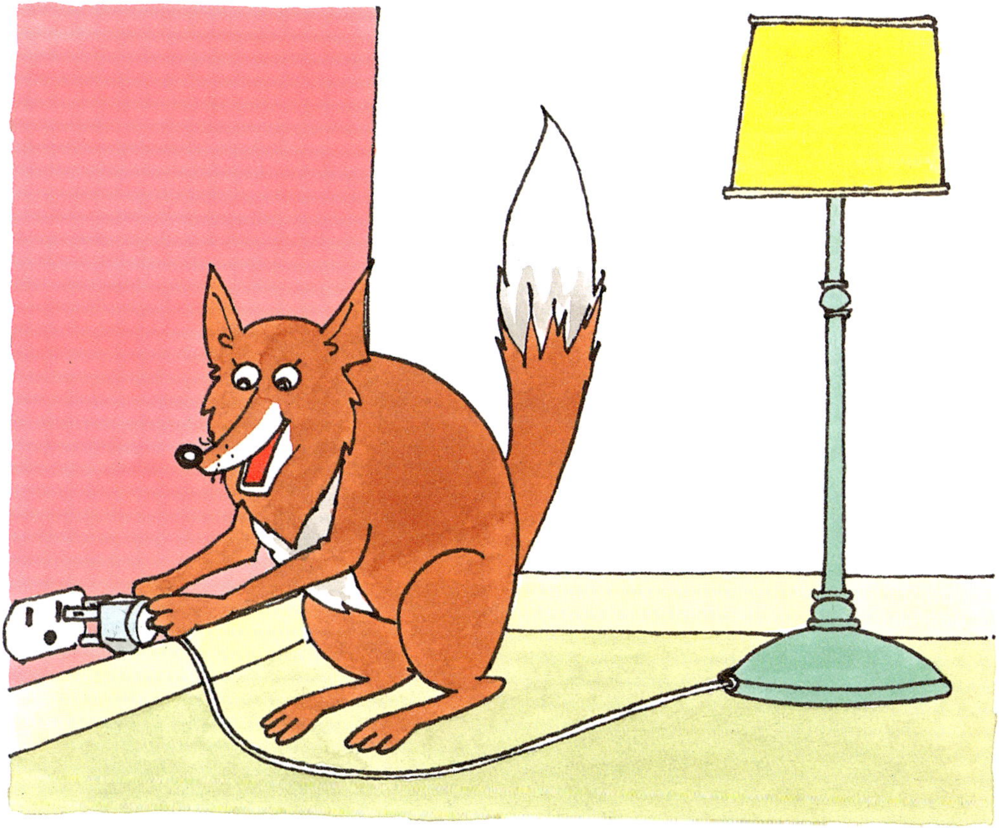

a plug

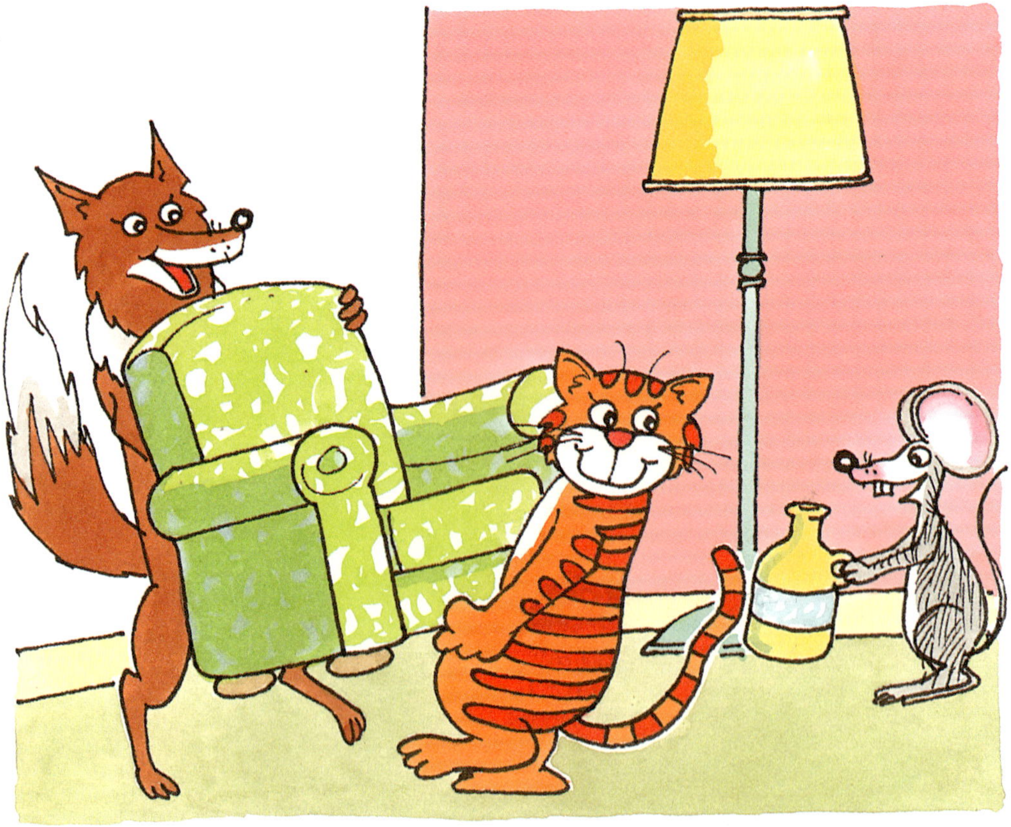

a jug

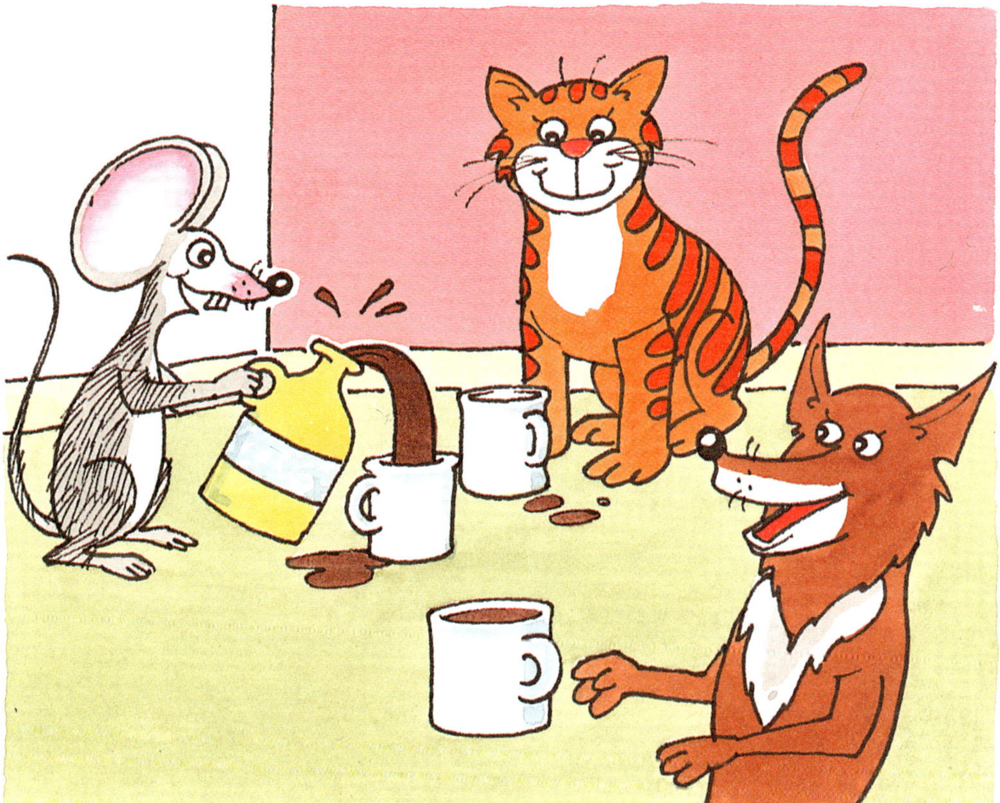

a mug

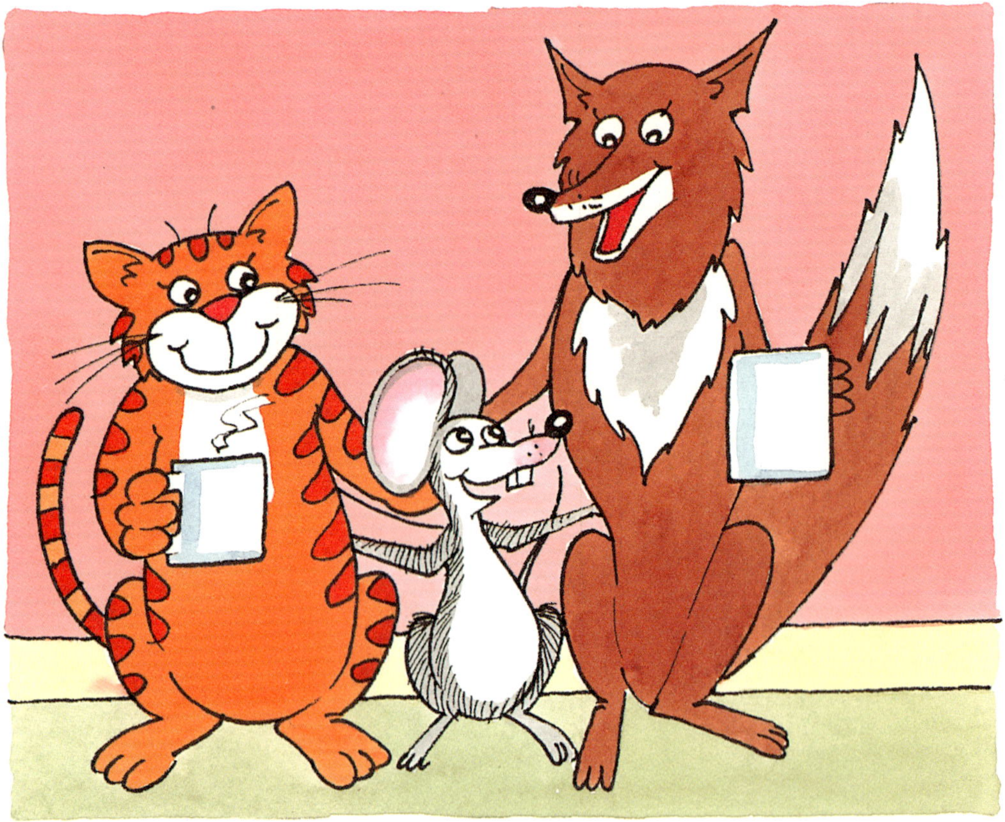

a hug